WILD about

FAST CARS

By David Kimber

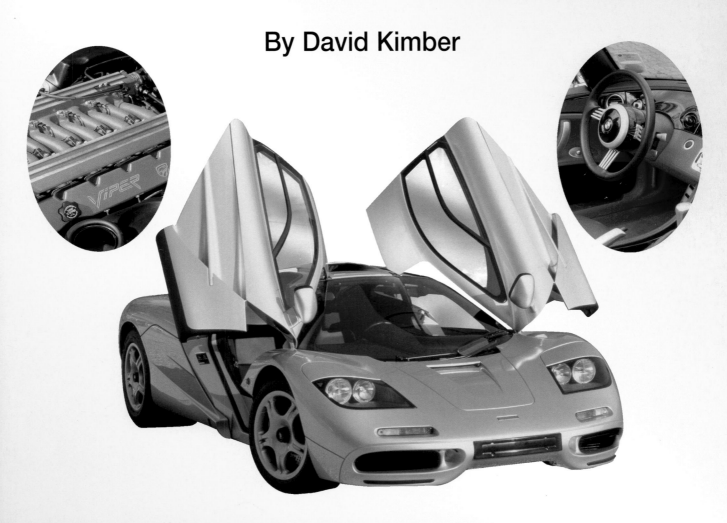

Stats and Facts • Top makes • Top models • Top speeds

WILD about
FAST CARS

Copyright © *ticktock* Entertainment Ltd 2006

First published in Great Britain in 2003 by *ticktock* Media Ltd.,
Unit 2, Orchard Business Centre, North Farm Road, Tunbridge Wells, Kent, TN2 3XF

We would like to thank: Tim Bones, Chris Lowe of *Fast Cars* magazine and Elizabeth Wiggans. All images Car Photo Library-www.carphoto.co.uk

ISBN 1 86007 358 1 HB
ISBN 1 86007 364 6 PB

Printed in Hong Kong

A CIP catalogue record for this book is available from the British Library.

CONTENTS

ASTON MARTIN V12 VANQUISH

The British firm Aston Martin made their first sports car back in 1914. Nearly ninety years later the **V12** Vanquish went on sale. With a powerful **engine** and a **body** made out of the lightweight metal **aluminium**, the four-seater Vanquish is one of the fastest cars in the world.

DID YOU KNOW?

In the film "Die Another Day", the super spy James Bond drives a V12 Vanquish.

The car has **tyre** pressure sensors, rain sensors and even sensors that switch the headlights on when it gets too dark.

The V12 has **Formula One**-style **gearchange paddles** behind the steering wheel. You click right to change up a **gear**, and left to change down.

The body panels are shaped by hand to make sure the edges are perfect.

BMW Z8

The Z8 is a modern sports car with old fashioned looks. This **roadster** is based on the beautiful BMW 507 built in the 1950s. Thanks to the enormous power from its **V8 engine**, the Z8 is more than just beautiful. Without the electronic speed reducer the top speed would be 180 mph.

The Z8 has a safety system called **Dynamic Stability Control** (**DSC**). If a corner is entered too quickly, the system stops the car going faster and **brakes** slow down all four wheels.

The dials are unusually placed in the centre of the **dashboard**. This gives the driver a clear view of the road.

Z8 customers can choose between a hard top or a soft top for their roadster.

DID YOU KNOW?

The Z8's satellite navigation system is hidden behind a flap in the dashboard.

BUGATTI EB 110

The Italian firm Bugatti was the biggest car maker in the world before it went bankrupt in the 1950s. Its famous name was brought back to life in 1987 and plans were made for a new car. Sadly Bugatti made just 356 EB 110's before they closed again in 1996.

The car was called the EB 110 because the founder of the company, Ettore Bugatti (EB), would have been 110 years old if he had lived to see it built.

The main **body** is a single **carbon fibre** unit. Left over units are being used in a new Italian supercar called the Edonis.

On the outside, the EB 110 looks like a car of the future. But inside it has a wooden **dashboard**, as you might find in an old sports car.

STATS AND FACTS

LAUNCHED: *1991*

ORIGIN: *Built in France*

ENGINE: *3,500 cc 60-valve V12, mid-mounted*

MAX POWER: *553 bhp at 8,000 rpm*

MAX TORQUE: *451 lb per ft at 3,250 rpm*

MAX SPEED: *209 mph*

ACCELERATION: *0-60 mph: 3.4 seconds*

WEIGHT: *1.56 tonnes*

COST: *£343,100*

DID YOU KNOW?

Ettore Bugatti was Italian but he spent most of his life in France and built his factory there.

CHEVROLET CORVETTE Z06

The American car company Chevrolet built their first Corvette in 1953. It soon became the world's most popular sports car. By 2002, millions of Corvettes had been sold all over the world. The reason for the car's success is simple. The Corvette is very fast but comes at a reasonable price.

DID YOU KNOW?

Over 200 of the earliest Corvettes have survived. They are now highly collectable.

In 1999 Chevrolet gave the Corvette a fighter plane-style display. Speed, **revolutions-per-minute** (**rpm**) and fuel levels are projected onto the windscreen.

This beautiful Corvette was built in 1960. Its powerful **V8 engine** gave a top speed of 130 mph. The average top speed of cars at that time was just 50 mph.

STATS AND FACTS

LAUNCHED: *1997*

ORIGIN: *USA*

ENGINE: *5,666 cc V8, front-mounted*

MAX POWER: *385 bhp at 6,000 rpm*

MAX TORQUE: *385 lb per ft at 4,800 rpm*

MAX SPEED: *175 mph*

ACCELERATION: *0-60 mph: 4 seconds*

WEIGHT: *1.41 tonnes*

COST: *£37,999*

Today the Corvette comes in three **body** styles. **Coupé** (hard top) for winter driving, **Targa** (with solid lift-out roof panel) and **Convertible** (soft top) for the summer.

CHRYSLER VIPER GTS

With twin stripes stretching right across its body, the Viper GTS looks as if it has arrived straight from the racetrack. This is because it was designed by Carol Shelby. He built the Shelby Cobras, racing cars that broke several records at the Daytona race circuit.

The Viper's enormous **V10 engine** was originally made for trucks. Chrysler gave the engine to Lamborghini, who gave it even more power – 450 **brake horse power (bhp).**

Before the GTS came the Dodge Viper. This car was only available in red or yellow. The GTS, however, comes in a range of colours, all with stripes.

DID YOU KNOW?

The Viper GTS had two entries in the Guinness Book of Records. One was for the fastest towing of a mobile home in 1998 and the other was for the fastest run by a blind driver in 1999.

STATS AND FACTS

LAUNCHED: *1996*

ORIGIN: *USA*

ENGINE: *7,990 cc V10, front-mounted*

MAX POWER: *378 bhp at 5,100 rpm*

MAX TORQUE: *454 lb per ft at 3,600 rpm*

MAX SPEED: *177 mph*

ACCELERATION: *0-60 mph: 4.5 seconds*

WEIGHT: *1.29 tonnes*

COST: *£68,825*

The massive amount of power from the V10 engine makes the GTS a challenge to drive fast even on dry roads. If it rains, leave your GTS at home because this Viper can bite!

FERRARI F50

Ferrari is one of the most famous makers of sports cars in the world. The F50 is one of the most exclusive models ever built. Just 349 cars were built to celebrate the Italian legend's 50th anniversary. This incredible car is powered by a slightly less powerful version of a 1990 **Formula One** engine.

TPV 16

The F50's **body**, doors and seats are made from lightweight **carbon fibre**.

Underneath the car the body is completely flat. The four **exhausts** stick out through holes cut into the rear, just like a racing car.

The engine is in the middle of the F50. It powers the Ferrari to 60 mph in under 4 seconds. The car goes from 0-100 mph in just 8 seconds and 0-150 mph in 18 seconds.

DID YOU KNOW?

The F50 is a very expensive car. But you still have to wind the windows up and down by hand!

JAGUAR XJ220S

In the late 1980s, the British car maker Jaguar decided to build a **supercar**. They called it the XJ220. In 1992 the first models were delivered to customers, costing £415,000 each. Two years later, Jaguar produced an even faster, lighter and cheaper version of the car. It was called the XJ220S.

DID YOU KNOW?

In 1994 racing driver Martin Brundle reached 217 mph in an XJ220S. At the time this was the fastest speed ever recorded by a road car.

The back of the car has an enormous wing. It stretches right across the body of one of the widest sports cars ever made.

The XJ220S was built by TWR (Tom Walkinshaw Racing). They based their design on the XJ220C cars that took part in the Le Mans race in France in 1993.

The XJ220's **aluminium** body was replaced with **carbon fibre** to make the XJ220S even lighter. The power was also increased from 542 **bhp** to 680 bhp.

LAMBORGHINI MURCIÉLAGO

Ferrucio Lamborghini was a millionaire tractor maker from northern Italy. Unhappy with the Ferrari he owned he decided he could build a better car himself. In 1966 Lamborghini made the first real **supercar**, the Miura. In 2001, the company started selling their tenth model, the Murciélago.

The roof and the doors of the Murciélago are made of steel. The rest of the car is made from **carbon fibre**.

DID YOU KNOW?

The Lamborghini badge features a charging bull, a symbol of both beauty and violence.

To reverse the Murciélago, most drivers flip open a door, and sit on the edge of the car. They can then look over their shoulder to see where they are going!

STATS AND FACTS

LAUNCHED: *2001*

ORIGIN: *Italy*

ENGINE: *6,192 cc V12, mid-mounted*

MAX POWER: *571 bhp at 7,500 rpm*

MAX TORQUE: *479 lb per ft at 5,400 rpm*

MAX SPEED: *205 mph*

ACCELERATION: *0-60 mph: 4 seconds*

WEIGHT: *1.65 tonnes*

COST: *£163,000*

The Murciélago is easier to drive than previous Lamborghinis. It has **four-wheel drive** and a safety system that slows the car down if it starts to lose its grip on the road.

McLAREN F1

McLaren are famous makers of **Formula One** cars. In 1993 the firm decided to make the ultimate **supercar**. The result was the F1. It was the first car costing one million dollars, and the fastest road car ever.

DID YOU KNOW?

An annual service for the McLaren F1 costs an amazing £25,000!

The back of the car is taken up by the huge BMW **engine**. It powers the F1 to 100 mph two seconds faster than a Ferrari, and on to a blistering 240 mph.

STATS AND FACTS

LAUNCHED: *1993*

ORIGIN: *UK*

ENGINE: *6,064 cc 48-valve V12, mid-mounted*

MAX POWER: *627 bhp at 7,400 rpm*

MAX TORQUE: *479 lb per ft at 7,000 rpm*

MAX SPEED: *240.1 mph*

ACCELERATION:
0-60 mph: 3.2 seconds
0-100 mph: 6.3 seconds

WEIGHT: *1.14 tonnes*

COST: *£634,500*

The F1's central driving position is unusual for a supercar. The two rear seats are also unusual for a sports car.

A total of 100 F1 road cars were built before McLaren stopped making them in 1998. Each one took nearly two months to build!

MERCEDES-BENZ SL500

The latest SL model from Mercedes-Benz is not cheap. However, it is one of the best value sports cars available. You can keep the roof up to stay dry in the winter, or press a button to change it into a **convertible**.

DID YOU KNOW?

One extra for the SL500 is a seat cushion with a built in massager!

A computer chip is used to unlock the car. Other special features include **satellite navigation**, a hi-fi and a TV monitor, all voice-activated!

The roof folds into the boot at the click of a button. It takes just 17 seconds for the top to come down.

STATS AND FACTS

LAUNCHED: *2001*

ORIGIN: *Germany*

ENGINE: *4,966 cc 24-valve V8, front-mounted*

MAX POWER: *302 bhp at 5,600 rpm*

MAX TORQUE: *339 lb per ft at 2,700 rpm*

MAX SPEED: *155 mph (limited)*

ACCELERATION: *0-60 mph: 6.3 seconds*

WEIGHT: *1.77 tonnes*

COST: *£68,000*

The SL500 was inspired by the 190 SL, built in 1956. This car was a classic Mercedes-Benz **roadster**. It was driven by Elvis Presley in the film "GI Blues".

PAGANI ZONDA C12 S

This car was designed by an Argentinian called Horacio Pagani. It is named after a wind that blows from the Andes mountains in Argentina. The Pagani Zonda is the newest and most exclusive **supercar**. There were only 30 built in the first year.

DID YOU KNOW?

When you buy a Zonda, you get a pair of driving shoes made for you by the Pope's shoe maker.

The Zonda has no boot at all! The only luggage space is behind the seats.

This C12 S model has a massive 7.3 litre **V12 engine**. It is made by AMG, who make racing car engines for Mercedes-Benz.

STATS AND FACTS

LAUNCHED: *2001*

ORIGIN: *Italy*

ENGINE: *7,010 cc V12, mid-mounted*

MAX POWER: *562 bhp at 5,500 rpm*

MAX TORQUE: *553 lb per ft at 4,100 rpm*

MAX SPEED: *220 mph*

ACCELERATION: *0-60 mph: 3.7 seconds*

WEIGHT: *1.25 tonnes*

COST: *£298,000*

The Zonda looks like a fighter plane. It has a glass-roofed cabin, twin **spoilers** and a rocket-style **exhaust**. The inside is made of **aluminium**, suede, leather and **carbon fibre**.

PORSCHE 911 GT2

On the outside the GT2 looks like an ordinary Porsche 911 Turbo. But inside all of the luxuries have been removed to make the car drive like a racing car. There is harder **suspension**, a **rollcage**, special **brakes** and a lot of extra power! The GT2 costs £30,000 more than the Turbo, but it is the fastest 911 ever.

DID YOU KNOW?

The GT2 is the fastest road car in Porsche's history, capable of 197 mph.

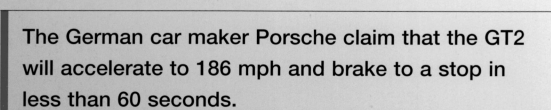

The German car maker Porsche claim that the GT2 will accelerate to 186 mph and brake to a stop in less than 60 seconds.

The rear wing and side panels have vents to cool the huge **engine**. There are also vents in the **nose** and slats in the bonnet. They direct air to cool the **radiator** and brakes.

The GT2 is 10 percent more powerful and 7 percent lighter than the 911 Turbo.

TVR TUSCAN

TVR are based in England. They have been making affordable sports cars for over forty years. In 2000 the firm started selling the Tuscan. They made the car as light as possible and gave it a huge **engine**. The result is an amazingly fast car that costs far less than its rivals.

DID YOU KNOW?

John Travolta drove a purple Tuscan in the 2001 film "Swordfish".

To get into the Tuscan, press a little button under the wing mirror. To get out, twist a knob inside the car.

The roof and the rear window can be taken off and stored in the Tuscan's large boot. There is even enough space left over for a couple of suitcases!

STATS AND FACTS

LAUNCHED: *2000*

ORIGIN: *UK*

ENGINE: *3,605 cc 24 valve Inline 6, front-mounted*

MAX POWER: *350 bhp at 7,200 rpm*

MAX TORQUE: *290 lb per ft at 5,500 rpm*

MAX SPEED: *180 mph*

ACCELERATION: *0-60 mph: 4.4 seconds*

WEIGHT: *1.1 tonnes*

COST: *£39,850*

The Tuscan's engine uses most of the space under the bonnet. It powers the car to 180 mph.

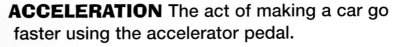

GLOSSARY

ACCELERATION The act of making a car go faster using the accelerator pedal.

BHP Brake horse power, the measure of an engine's power output.

BODY Outer part of a car that covers the chassis and engine.

BRAKES Part of a car used to slow it down.

CARBON FIBRE A modern lightweight material used to make cars.

CC Cubic capacity, the measurement used for the size of an engine.

CHASSIS The part which holds the engine, wheels and body together.

CONVERTIBLE (*See Roadster*).

COUPÉ A two-door hard top car.

CYLINDER The part of the engine where fuel is burned to make energy.

DASHBOARD The panel behind the steering wheel that usually contains the speedometer and other dials.

DYNAMIC STABILITY CONTROL A driver aid which can safely brake any or all four wheels.

ENGINE The part of the car where fuel is burned to create energy.

EXHAUST Pipe at the back of the car that lets out poisonous gases made when petrol is burned. The exhaust is also used to reduce engine noise.

FORMULA ONE Famous motor racing championship.

FOUR-WHEEL DRIVE A car that has power delivered to all four wheels.

GEARS System used to allow a car to go faster or slower safely without damaging the engine.

GEARCHANGE PADDLES Levers on a steering wheel used to change up and down gears.

NOSE The front end of a car.

RADIATOR A device through which water or other fluids flow to keep the engine cool.

ROADSTER A car with a roof that can be folded back or removed.

ROLLCAGE A metal framework within a car to prevent crushing in the event of a car turning over in a crash.

RPM Revolutions (revs) of the engine per minute.

SATELLITE NAVIGATION A system which tells you where your car is and lets you plot a route to any destination.

SPOILER A lightweight panel attached to a car to prevent the vehicle lifting up at high speeds.

SUPERCAR A high performance, high cost road car.

SUSPENSION Springs and shock absorbers attached to a car's wheels, giving a smooth ride even on bumpy surfaces.

TAIL The rear of the car.

TARGA A hard top car with a removable roof panel.

TORQUE The force with which engine power can be delivered to a car's wheels.

TRACTION CONTROL A driver aid that helps tyres grip the road.

TYRE A rubber wheel covering filled with compressed air.

V8/V12 The engine size given in number of cylinders.

V/INLINE/FLAT The arrangement of the cylinders in the engine.

VALVE Device that controls the flow of petrol into the engine.

INDEX